DIY MONSTERS & MISCHIEF MAKERSPACE

MAKE A CREEPY COSTUME YOUR WAY!

ELSIE OLSON

CONSULTING EDITOR,
DIANE CRAIG,
M.A./READING SPECIALIST

Super Sandcastle

An Imprint of Abdo Publishing
abdobooks.com

abdobooks.com

Published by Abdo Publishing, a division of ABDO, PO Box 398166, Minneapolis, Minnesota 55439. Copyright © 2021 by Abdo Consulting Group, Inc. International copyrights reserved in all countries. No part of this book may be reproduced in any form without written permission from the publisher. Super SandCastle™ is a trademark and logo of Abdo Publishing.

Printed in the United States of America, North Mankato, Minnesota
052020
092020

THIS BOOK CONTAINS
RECYCLED MATERIALS

Design: Emily O'Malley, Mighty Media, Inc.
Production: Mighty Media, Inc.
Editor: Megan Borgert-Spaniol
Cover Photographs: Mighty Media, Inc.; Shutterstock Images
Interior Photographs: Mighty Media, Inc.; Shutterstock Images

The following manufacturers/names appearing in this book are trademarks:
Adhesive Tech™, Elmer's® Glue-All®, Market Pantry™

Library of Congress Control Number: 2019957511

Publisher's Cataloging-in-Publication Data
Names: Olson, Elsie, author.
Title: Make a creepy costume your way! / by Elsie Olson
Description: Minneapolis, Minnesota : Abdo Publishing, 2021 | Series: DIY monsters & mischief makerspace | Includes online resources and index.
Identifiers: ISBN 9781532193163 (lib. bdg.) | ISBN 9781098211806 (ebook)
Subjects: LCSH: Handicraft for children--Juvenile literature. | Costume design--Juvenile literature. | Textile crafts--Juvenile literature. | Monsters--Juvenile literature. | Paper work--Juvenile literature. | Refuse as art material--Juvenile literature.
Classification: DDC 745.5--dc23

Super SandCastle™ books are created by a team of professional educators, reading specialists, and content developers around five essential components—phonemic awareness, phonics, vocabulary, text comprehension, and fluency—to assist young readers as they develop reading skills and strategies and increase their general knowledge. All books are written, reviewed, and leveled for guided reading and early reading intervention programs for use in shared, guided, and independent reading and writing activities to support a balanced approach to literacy instruction.

TO ADULT HELPERS

The projects in this book are fun and simple. There are just a few things to remember to keep kids safe. Some projects may use sharp or hot objects. Also, kids may be using messy supplies. Make sure they protect their clothes and work surfaces. Be ready to offer guidance during brainstorming and assist when necessary.

CONTENTS

BECOME A MAKER

A makerspace is like a laboratory. It's a place where ideas are formed and problems are solved. Kids like you create wonderful things in makerspaces. Many makerspaces are in schools and libraries. But they can also be in kitchens, bedrooms, and backyards. Anywhere can be a makerspace when you use imagination, inspiration, **collaboration**, and problem-solving!

IMAGINATION

This takes you to new places and lets you experience new things. Anything is possible with imagination!

INSPIRATION

This is the spark that gives you an idea. Inspiration can come from almost anywhere!

Makerspace Toolbox

COLLABORATION

Makers work together. They ask questions and get ideas from everyone around them. **Collaboration** solves problems that seem impossible.

PROBLEM–SOLVING

Things often don't go as planned when you're creating. But that's part of the fun! Find creative **solutions** to any problem that comes up. These will make your project even better.

MAKE SOME MISCHIEF!

When was the last time you made mischief? Mischief is playful behavior that's goofy or surprising. Mischief can take the form of a funny **prank** or teasing trick. You can also make mischief with a creepy costume that spooks or shocks others!

PROBLEM-SOLVE!
See page 26

THRILLS AND CHILLS

People wear costumes when they want to pretend to be someone or something else. Costumes can be funny, realistic, pretty, or creepy. Creepy costumes can be especially exciting to wear. It's fun to see how people react when they see a creepy costume!

IMAGINE A CREEPY COSTUME

When you think of a creepy costume, you might think of a monster. You've probably seen lots of monsters in movies, books, and TV shows. Werewolves, vampires, and ghosts are all popular monsters. But when you are in a makerspace, you can create any type of creepy costume your imagination can dream up!

GET INSPIRED!
See page 24

IMAGINE

If you could **design** any creepy costume, what would it look like? How might you use it to make mischief? Would you jump out and scare someone? Would you **lurk** in a dark corner? Or would you try to trick others with a **disguise**? Remember, there are no rules. Let your imagination run wild!

DESIGN A CREEPY COSTUME

It's time to turn your idea into a makerspace marvel! Think about the creepy costume you imagined. Did it cover your entire body? Did it include **accessories** such as belts, hats, or crowns? How could you use the materials around you to create the features of your costume? Where would you begin?

INSPIRATION

Every Halloween, haunted houses pop up around the world. These buildings are filled with spooky sets and actors dressed in creepy costumes. People visit haunted houses at night to get scared silly. Many haunted houses also offer lights-on tours. Kids can see the cool sets and costumes without getting too scared!

COLLABORATE!
See page 28

BE SAFE, BE RESPECTFUL
MAKERSPACE ETIQUETTE

THERE ARE JUST A FEW RULES TO FOLLOW WHEN YOU ARE CREATING YOUR CREEPY COSTUME:

1. **ASK FOR PERMISSION AND ASK FOR HELP.** Make sure an adult says it's OK to make your costume. Get help when using sharp tools, such as a craft knife, or hot tools, like a glue gun.

2. **THINK IT THROUGH.** Don't give up when things don't work out exactly right. Instead, think about the problem you are having. What are some ways to solve it?

3. **SHARE THE SPACE.** Share supplies and space with other makers. Put materials away when you are finished working. Find a safe space to store unfinished projects until next time.

4. **BE NICE.** Keep your tricks and **pranks** fun or funny, but not mean. Don't make your creepy costume too scary for your audience. Mischief should be fun for everyone!

WHAT WILL YOUR COSTUME DO?

How will you use your creepy costume to make mischief? Knowing this will help you figure out which materials to use.

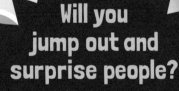

Will you jump out and surprise people?
Then your costume will need to be **flexible** and sturdy.

PROBLEM-SOLVE!
See page 26

IMAGINE

THINK ABOUT THE CREEPIEST MOVIE MONSTER YOU'VE SEEN. WHAT FEATURES MADE IT SO CREEPY? COULD YOU USE SIMILAR FEATURES IN YOUR COSTUME?

Will you use your costume to trick people? Then you'll need a mask or makeup for your **disguise**.

13

MEET A MAKER

Marina Toybina is the costume **designer** for *The Masked Singer*. This popular show features stars performing songs in full-body costumes. Toybina's costumes include monsters, animals, and more!

Will you gross people out with a second head?

Then you'll need a sturdy strap to attach it to your body.

COLLABORATE!
See page 28

Will you fool people into thinking they've seen a ghost? Then you'll need a material thick enough to hide your face, but thin enough to see through.

⚠ STUCK?

YOU CAN ALWAYS CHANGE YOUR MIND IN A MAKERSPACE. IF YOUR SECOND HEAD ISN'T LOOKING CREEPY ENOUGH, THROW A SHEET OVER IT TO MAKE A SHOULDER GHOST!

15

CRAFT YOUR COSTUME

A good costume is comfortable and safe to wear. It should also be **adjustable** so it fits you just right. Keep in mind how much you'll move around in it. **Flexible** materials can be shaped to fit your body. They won't fall apart as you make mischief!

► SEARCH YOUR SPACE ◄

The perfect material might be in a kitchen drawer, your school desk, or even your closet. Search for materials that might seem surprising!

GET INSPIRED!
See page 24

FABRIC

CELLOPHANE

COMFY & CUTTABLE

POOL NOODLE

FELT MASK

FIRM & FLEXIBLE

FELT HAT

ALUMINUM PIE TIN

STIFF & STURDY

CONNECT YOUR COSTUME

Will you keep your costume for a long time? Or will you take it apart after you are done wearing it? Knowing this will help you decide what materials to use.

TOTALLY TEMPORARY

| STRAIGHT PINS | HOOK-AND-LOOP TAPE | THUMBTACKS | KNOTTED NYLON STRAP |

COLLABORATE!
See page 28

IMAGINE

WHAT IF YOU WANTED TO MAKE A MATCHING CREEPY COSTUME FOR YOUR PET? WHAT FEATURES WOULD YOU NEED TO ADAPT?

A LITTLE STICKY

SUPER STICKY

CRAFT GLUE

GLUE DOTS

DUCT TAPE

HOT GLUE

19

DECORATE YOUR COSTUME

Decorating is the final step in making your creepy costume. It's where you add **details** to trick and surprise people. How do these decorations help bring your costume to life?

REALISTIC BITS

LEAVES AND BARK

MOSS

IMAGINE

IMAGINE YOUR CREEPY COSTUME CAME TO LIFE. HOW WOULD IT MOVE? WHAT SOUNDS MIGHT IT MAKE? CAN YOU INCLUDE THESE DETAILS WHEN YOU WEAR YOUR COSTUME?

GET INSPIRED!
See page 24

THRILLING TRICKS

GRIM & GHASTLY

CELLOPHANE

FAKE BUGS

PAINT AND GLUE
MIXTURE

PING-PONG BALLS

HELPFUL HACKS

As you work, you might discover ways to make challenging tasks easier. Try these simple tricks and **techniques** as you craft your costume!

Soak cotton or wool in paint mixed with water. Let it dry. Then cut it into pieces to create moss.

Mix flour and water to make a sticky paste. Use the paste to layer strips of newspaper around a **mold**. Let it dry for 24 hours, and then remove it from your mold.

PROBLEM-SOLVE!
See page 26

Cut an aluminum pie tin to make a crown. Make cuts with a craft knife and weave in thin metal strips for spikes.

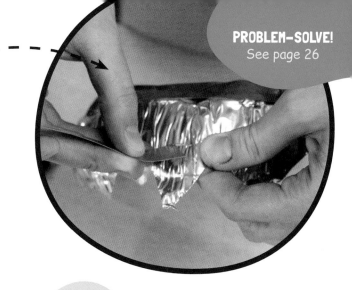

Combine glue, paint, and cornstarch to create raised scars on a mask.

⚠ STUCK?

MAKERS AROUND THE WORLD SHARE THEIR PROJECTS ON THE INTERNET AND IN BOOKS. IF YOU HAVE A MAKERSPACE PROBLEM, THERE'S A GOOD CHANCE SOMEONE ELSE HAS ALREADY FOUND A SOLUTION. SEARCH THE INTERNET OR LIBRARY FOR HELPFUL ADVICE AS YOU MAKE YOUR PROJECTS!

23

GET INSPIRED

Get inspiration from the real world before you start creating your creepy costume!

LOOK AT NATURE

Nature is full of creepy-crawly plants and animals. The Venus flytrap is a plant with terrifying teeth! The Goliath bird-eating spider can grow as large as a dinner plate. And explorers once thought Komodo dragons were real-life monsters!

LOOK AT LEGENDS

Humans around the world have been telling monster stories for thousands of years. Ask an adult to help you search online for monster **legends**. You can learn about sea monsters, Bigfoot, the chupacabra, and more!

LOOK AT FASHION

Costumes are a form of fashion. And many fashion **designers** come up with wild ideas! Look at style magazines, clothing **catalogs**, and pictures from fashion shows. What looks can you borrow for your creepy costume?

25

PROBLEM-SOLVE

No makerspace project goes exactly as planned. But with a little creativity, you can find a **solution** to any problem.

FIGURE OUT THE PROBLEM

Maybe you are having trouble removing your paper head from its **mold**. Why do you think this is happening? Thinking about what is causing the problem can lead you to a solution!

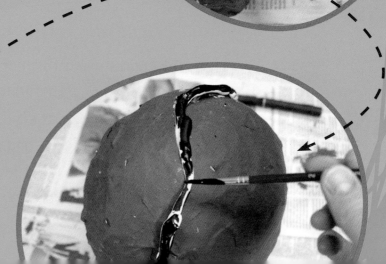

SOLUTION:
USE A CRAFT KNIFE TO CUT THE HEAD FROM THE MOLD. THEN USE GLUE AND CLAY TO FUSE THE HEAD BACK TOGETHER. PAINT THE CLAY TO TURN IT INTO A CREEPY SCAR!

BRAINSTORM AND TEST

Try coming up with three possible **solutions** to any problem.

Maybe your fake head isn't staying on your shoulder. You could:

1. Add more straps to secure the head to your body.

2. Use a new **technique** to attach the strap to the head.

3. Strap the head to a different part of your body!

COLLABORATE

Collaboration means working together with others. There are tons of ways to collaborate to create a creepy costume!

ASK A FELLOW MAKER

Don't be shy about asking a friend or classmate for help on your project. Other makers can help you think through the different steps to creating your creepy costume. These helpers can also lend a pair of hands during construction!

ASK AN ADULT HELPER

This could be a parent, teacher, grandparent, or any trusted adult. Tell this person how you would like to use your creepy costume to make mischief. Your grown-up helper might think of materials or **techniques** you never would have thought of!

ASK AN EXPERT

Does your school or community have a theater group? Ask the costume **designer** how to create striking and sturdy costumes for the stage!

THE WORLD IS A MAKERSPACE!

Your costume may look complete, but don't close your makerspace toolbox yet. Think about what would make your costume even creepier. What would you do differently if you made it again? What would happen if you used different **techniques** or materials?

IMAGINATION

INSPIRATION

COLLABORATION

PROBLEM-SOLVING

DON'T STOP AT COSTUMES

You can use your makerspace toolbox beyond the makerspace! You might use it to accomplish everyday tasks, such as mending ripped jeans or making a uniform for Spanish club. But makers use the same toolbox to do big things. One day, these tools could help humans travel the solar system or swim deep in the ocean. Turn your world into a makerspace! What problems could you solve?

GLOSSARY

accessory – a piece of jewelry or clothing that makes an outfit appear more complete.

adjust – to change something slightly to produce a desired result. An object is adjustable if it is designed to be used in more than one way.

catalog – a book that shows items you can buy from a particular store.

collaborate – to work with others.

design – to plan how something will appear or work.

detail – a small part of something.

disguise – an appearance that is taken on to prevent recognition.

flexible – easy to move or bend.

legend – a story passed down through history that may not be true.

lurk – to wait in a somewhat hidden place.

mold – a form or frame around which something is constructed.

prank – a trick done to someone as a joke.

solution – an answer to, or a way to solve, a problem.

technique – a method or style in which something is done.